POP PIANO HITS

SIMPLE ARRANGEMENTS FOR STUDENTS OF ALL AGES

Drivers License, Willow & More Hot Singles

ISBN 978-1-70513-700-0

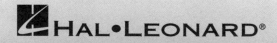

Visit Hal Leonard Online at
www.halleonard.com

Contact us:
Hal Leonard
7777 West Bluemound Road
Milwaukee, WI 53213
Email: info@halleonard.com

In Europe, contact:
Hal Leonard Europe Limited
42 Wigmore Street
Marylebone, London, W1U 2RN
Email: info@halleonardeurope.com

In Australia, contact:
Hal Leonard Australia Pty. Ltd.
4 Lentara Court
Cheltenham, Victoria, 3192 Australia
Email: info@halleonard.com.au

AFTERGLOW

Words and Music by ED SHEERAN,
DAVID HODGES and FRED GIBSON

Moderately fast

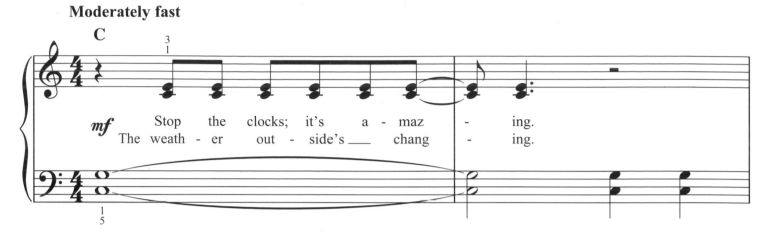

Stop the clocks; it's a-maz - ing.
The weath - er out - side's __ chang - ing.

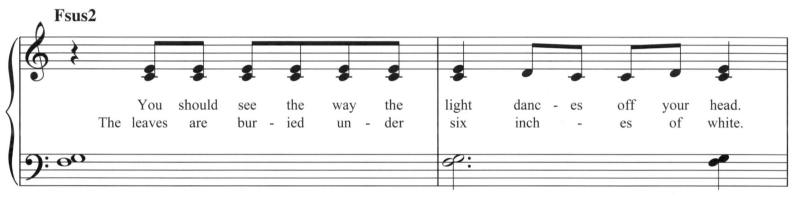

You should see the way the light danc - es off your head.
The leaves are bur - ied un - der six inch - es of white.

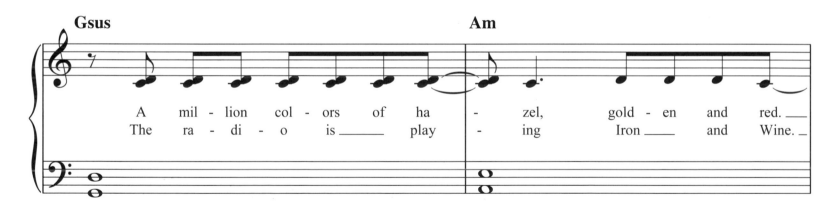

A mil - lion col - ors of ha - zel, gold - en and red.
The ra - di - o is __ play - ing Iron __ and Wine. __

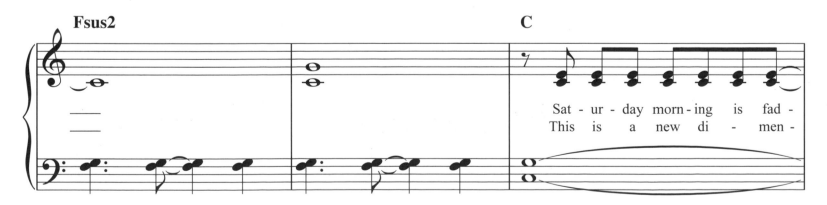

Sat - ur - day morn - ing is fad -
This is a new di - men -

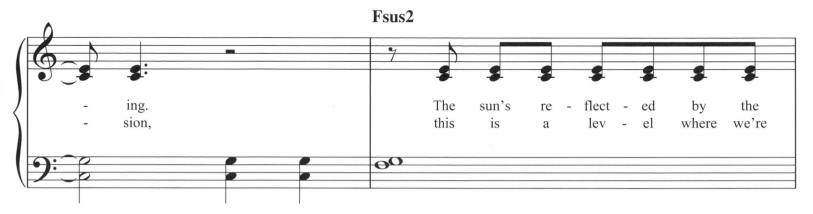

Fsus2

-ing.
-sion,

The sun's re-flect-ed by the
this is a lev-el where we're

Gsus

cof-fee in your hand.
los-ing track of time.

My eyes are caught in your gaze___
I'm hold-ing noth-ing a-gainst___

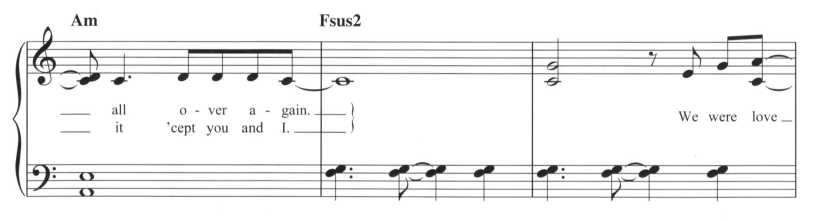

Am   **Fsus2**

___ all o-ver a-gain.___
___ it 'cept you and I.___

We were love ___

C

___ drunk, wait-ing on a mir-a-cle, ___ tryin' to find ___ our-selves in the

4

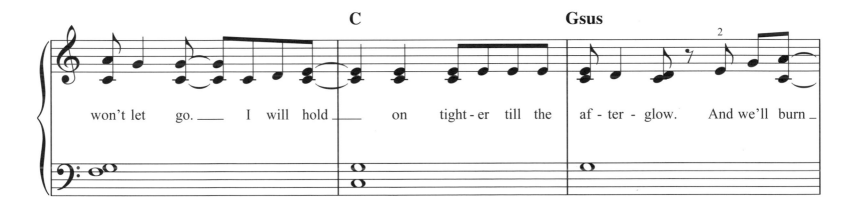

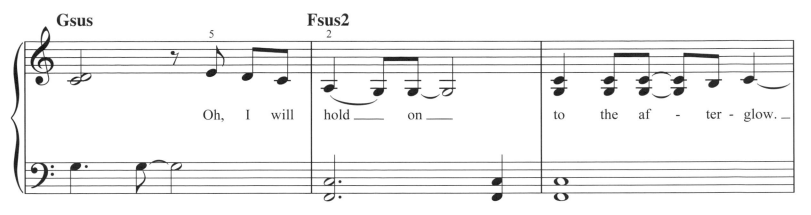

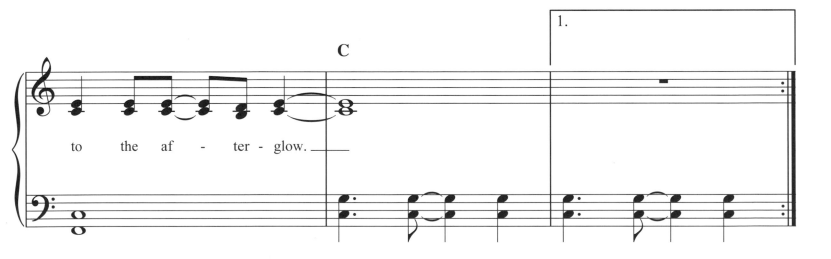

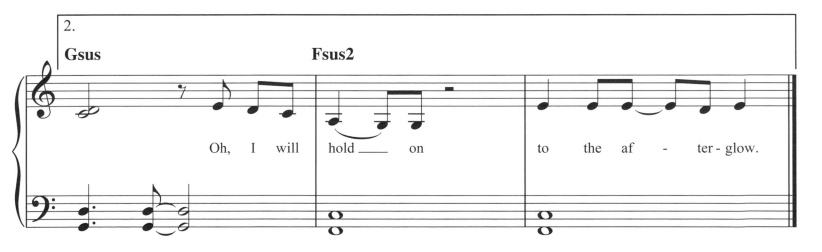

BLINDING LIGHTS

Words and Music by ABEL TESFAYE,
MAX MARTIN, JASON QUENNEVILLE,
OSCAR HOLTER and AHMAD BALSHE

Fast dance beat

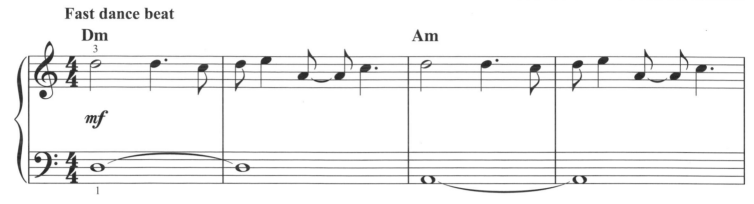

I've been try-na

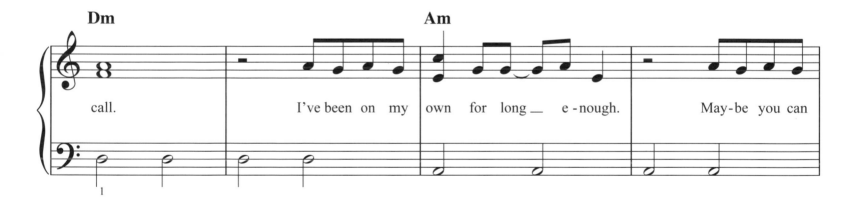

call. I've been on my own for long_ e-nough. May-be you can

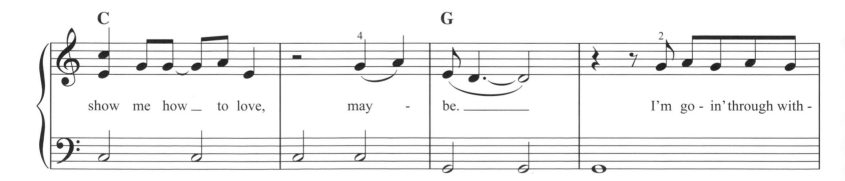

show me how_ to love, may - be. _____ I'm go-in' through with-

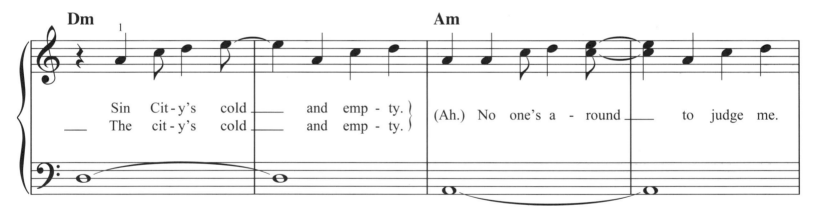

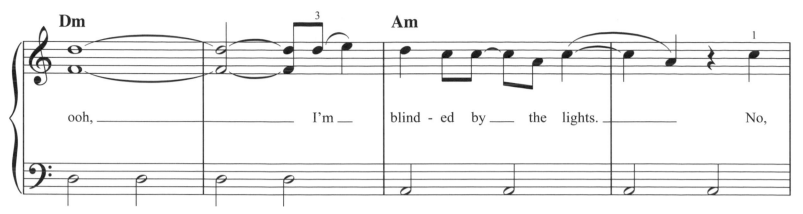

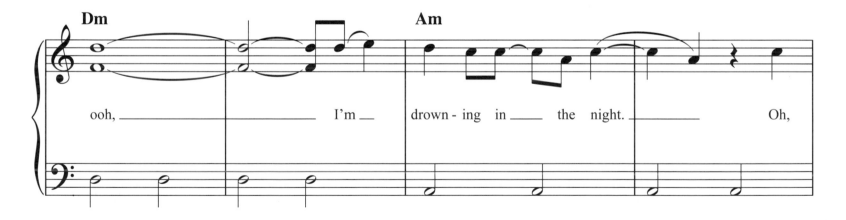

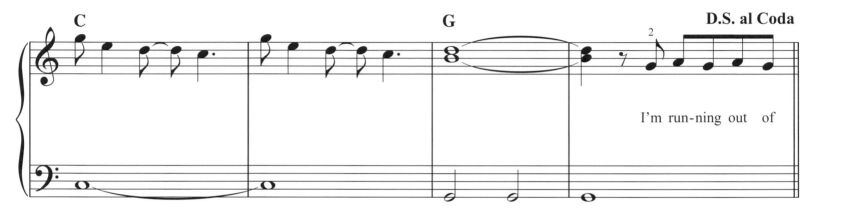

I'm run-ning out of

you're the one ___ I ___ trust.   I'm just walk-in'

by to let ___ you know, ___   I could nev - er   say   it on ___ the phone. ___   Will

never let you go this time.   I said,

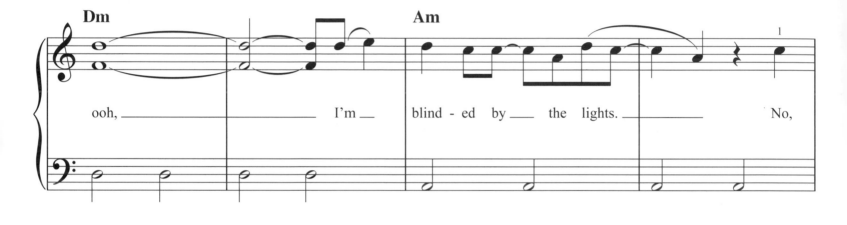

ooh,   I'm   blind-ed by   the lights.   No,

I can't sleep un - til I feel   your   touch. (Hey,   hey,   hey.)

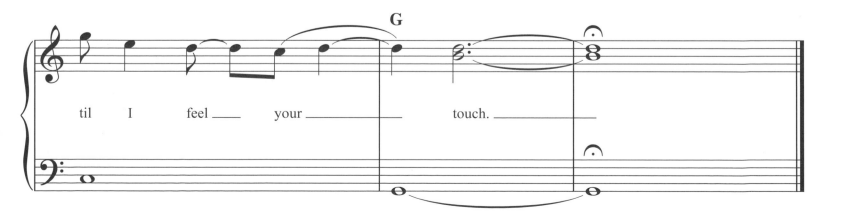

DRIVERS LICENSE

Words and Music by DANIEL NIGRO
and OLIVIA RODRIGO

Moderately slow

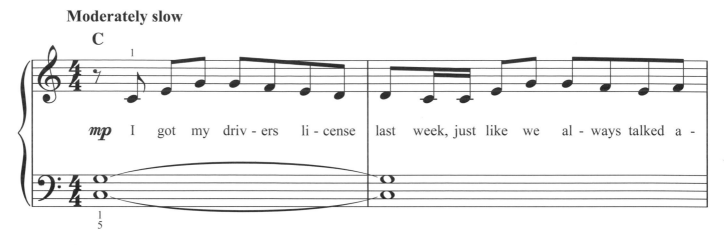

I got my driv-ers li-cense last week, just like we al-ways talked a-

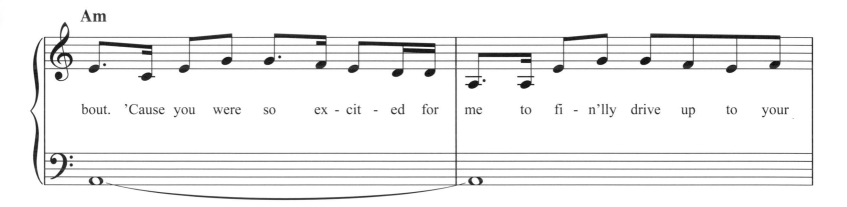

bout. 'Cause you were so ex-cit-ed for me to fi-n'lly drive up to your

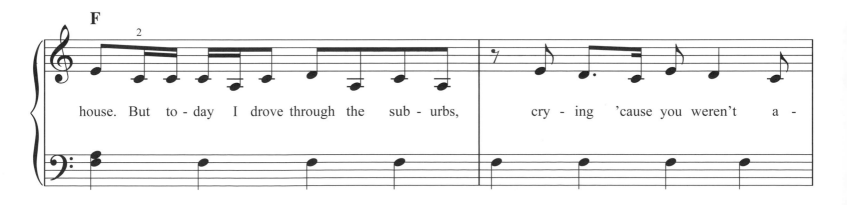

house. But to-day I drove through the sub-urbs, cry-ing 'cause you weren't a-

round.

And you're prob - 'ly   with   that   blond   girl

who   al - ways   made   me   doubt.

She's   so   much   old - er   than   me;   she's

ev - 'ry - thing I'm   in - se - cure   a - bout. Yeah, to -   day   I   drove through the   sub - urbs,

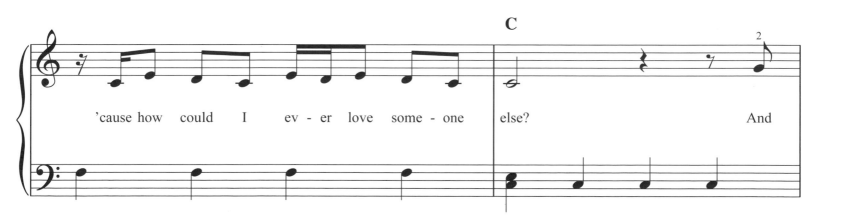

'cause how   could   I   ev - er   love   some - one

else?

And

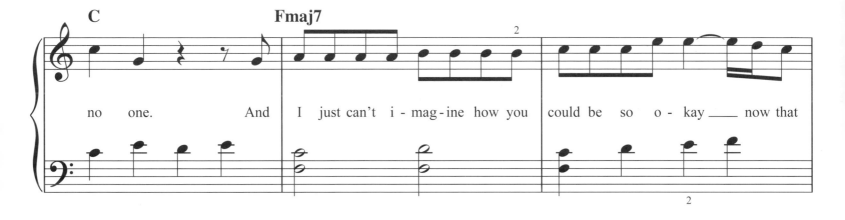

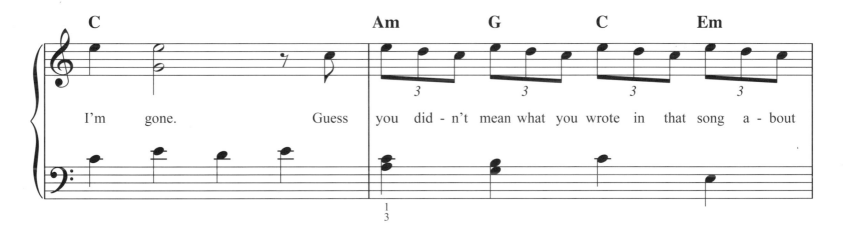

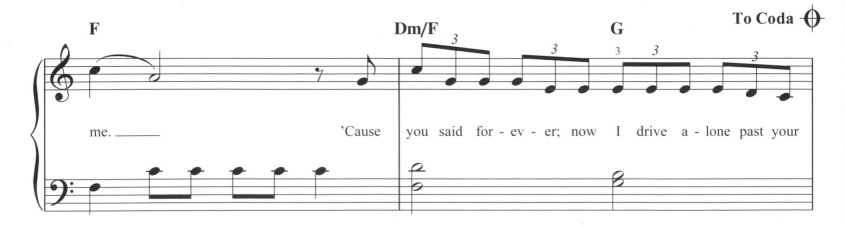

C

street. And all my friends are tired _____

Am

of hear-ing how much I miss you; but I kind of feel sor - ry for them, 'cause

F

they'll nev - er know you the way that I do. Yeah, to - day I drove through the sub - urbs and

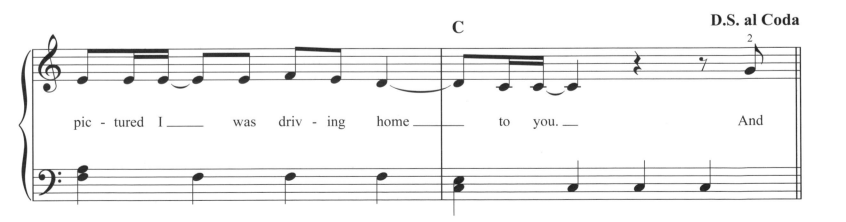

C **D.S. al Coda**

pic - tured I _____ was driv - ing home _____ to you. _____ And

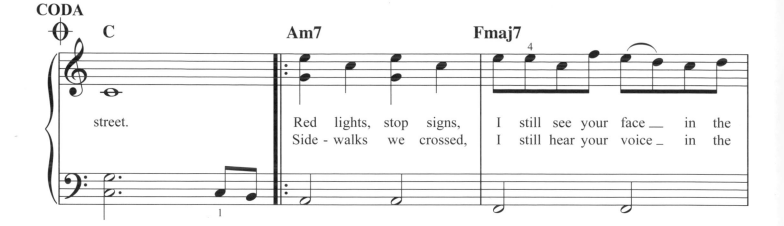

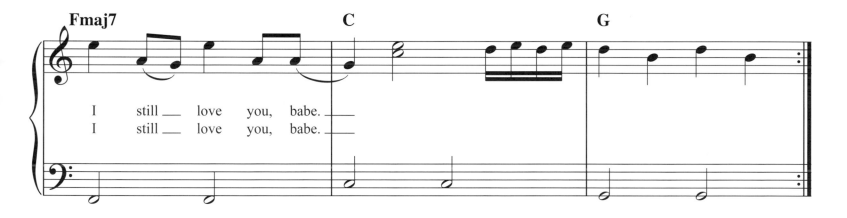

I just can't i-mag-ine how you could be so o-kay ___ now that I'm gone. Guess

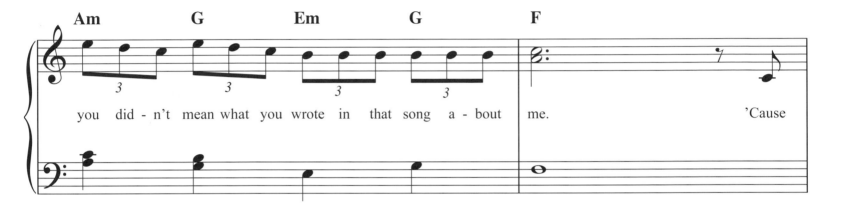

you did-n't mean what you wrote in that song a-bout me. 'Cause

you said for-ev-er; now I drive a-lone past your street. Yeah,

you said for-ev-er; now I drive a-lone past your street.

HOLY

Words and Music by JUSTIN BIEBER,
JON BELLION, ANTHONY JONES,
TOMMY BROWN, STEVEN FRANKS,
MICHAEL POLLACK, JORGEN ODEGARD
and CHANCELOR BENNETT

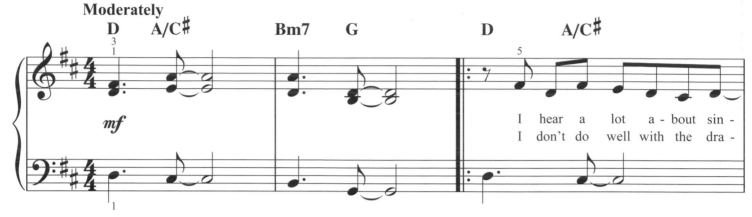

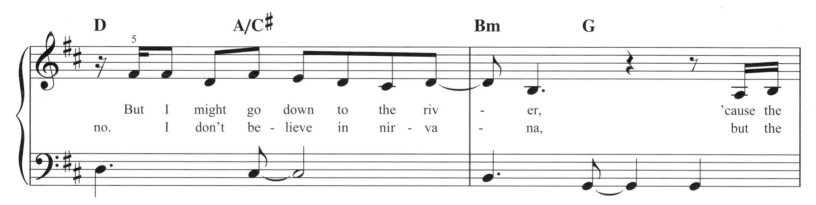

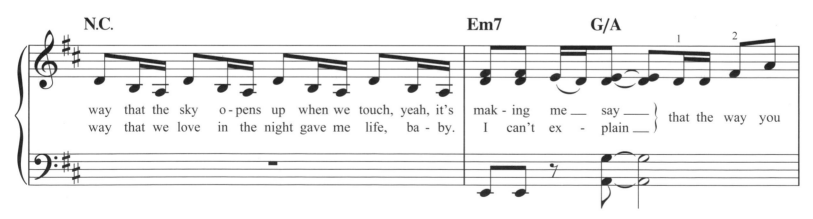

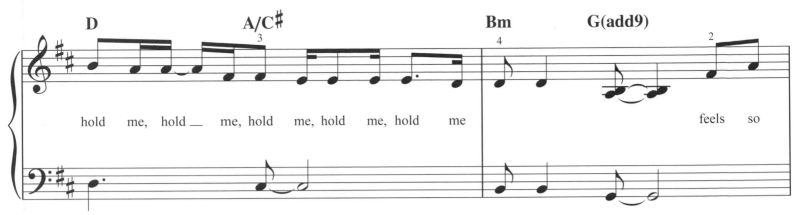

hold me, hold — me, hold me, hold me, hold me   feels so

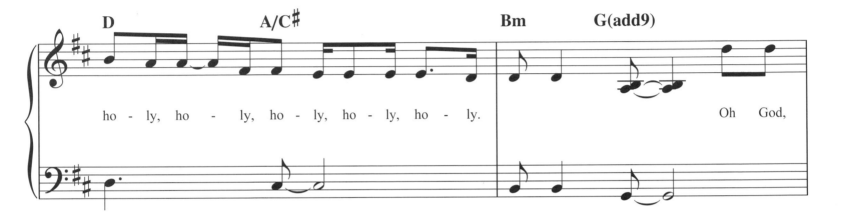

ho - ly, ho - ly, ho - ly, ho - ly, ho - ly.   Oh God,

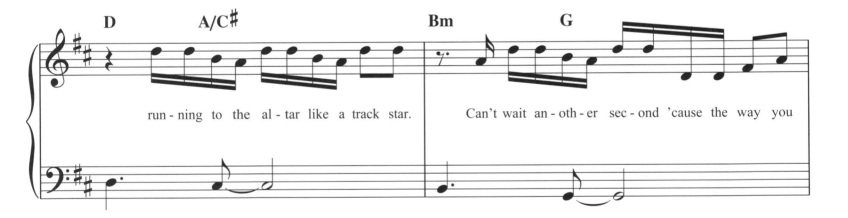

run - ning to the al - tar like a track star.   Can't wait an - oth - er sec - ond 'cause the way you

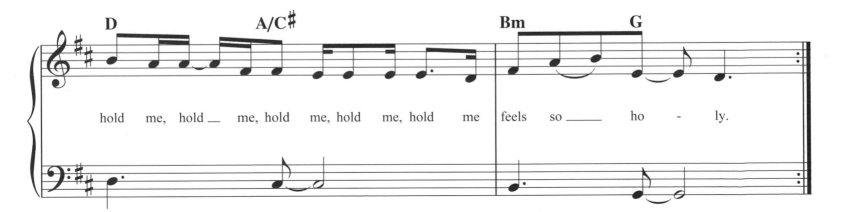

hold me, hold — me, hold me, hold me, hold me feels so _____ ho - ly.

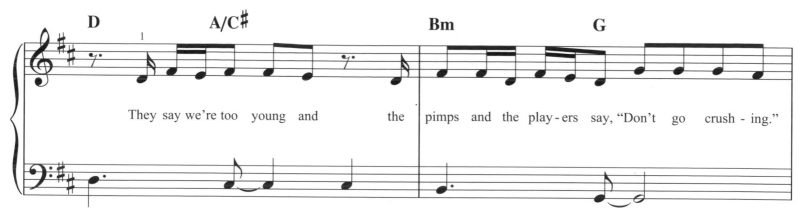

They say we're too young and the pimps and the play-ers say, "Don't go crush-ing."

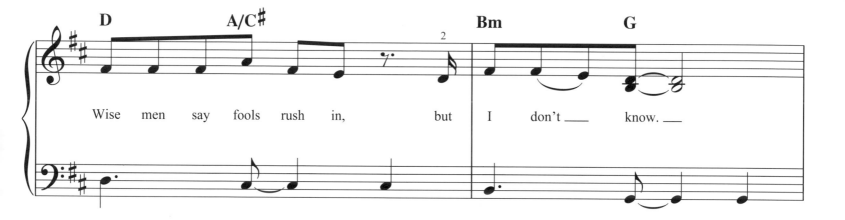

Wise men say fools rush in, but I don't ___ know. ___

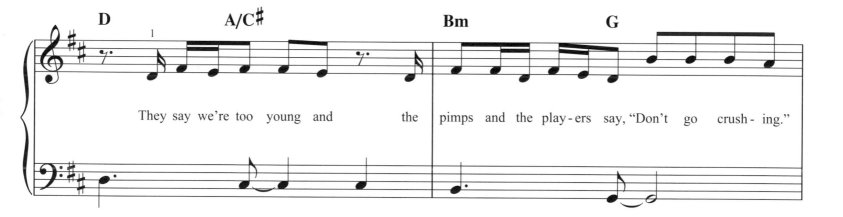

They say we're too young and the pimps and the play-ers say, "Don't go crush-ing."

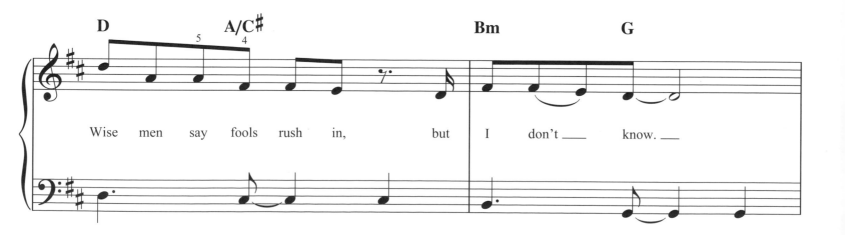

Wise men say fools rush in, but I don't ___ know. ___

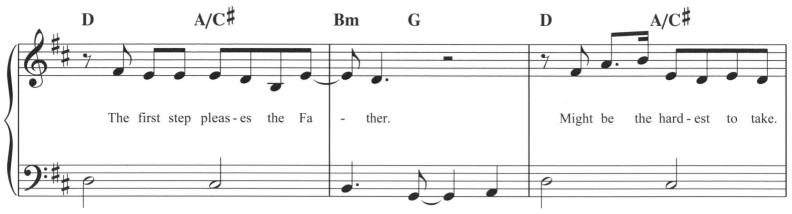

The first step pleas-es the Fa - ther. Might be the hard-est to take.

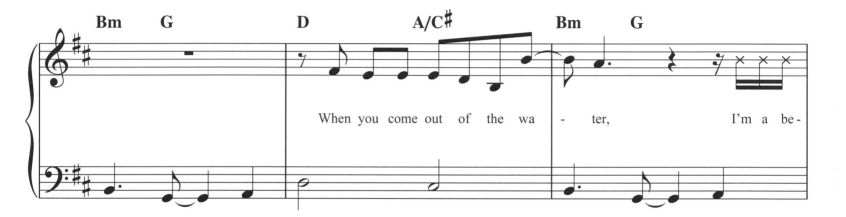

When you come out of the wa - ter, I'm a be-

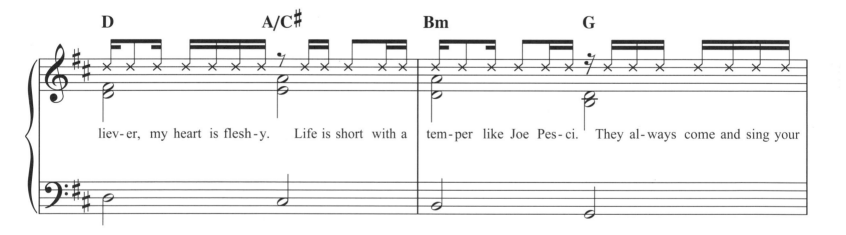

liev-er, my heart is flesh-y. Life is short with a tem-per like Joe Pes-ci. They al-ways come and sing your

prais-es, your name is catch-y. But they don't see you how I see you, Par-lay and De-si. Cross, Tween, Tween,

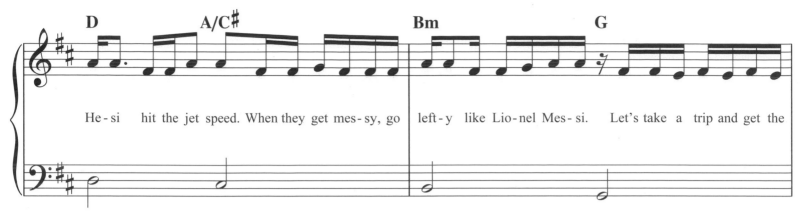

He-si hit the jet speed. When they get mes-sy, go | left-y like Lio-nel Mes-si.   Let's take a trip and get the

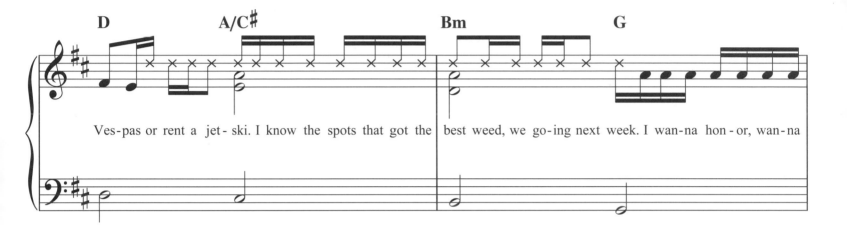

Ves-pas or rent a jet-ski. I know the spots that got the | best weed, we go-ing next week. I wan-na hon-or, wan-na

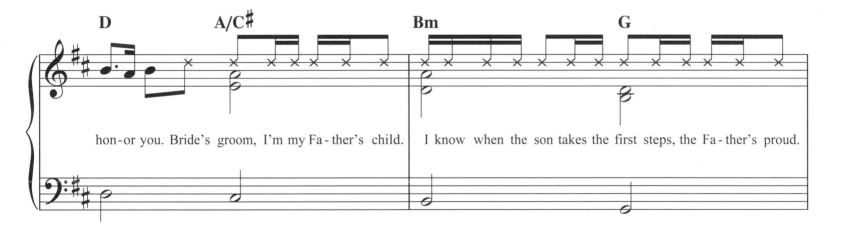

hon-or you. Bride's groom, I'm my Fa-ther's child. | I know when the son takes the first steps, the Fa-ther's proud.

If you make it to the wa-ter, He'll part the clouds. | I know he made you a snack like Os-car Proud.

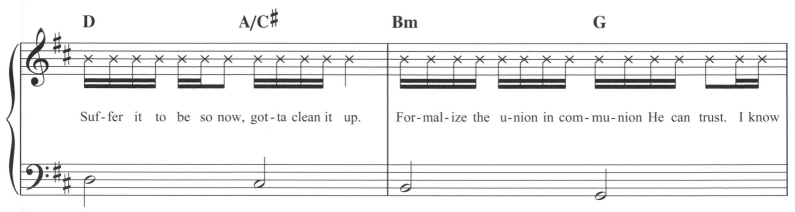

D   **A/C#**   **Bm**   **G**

Suf-fer it to be so now, got-ta clean it up.   For-mal-ize the u-nion in com-mu-nion He can trust. I know

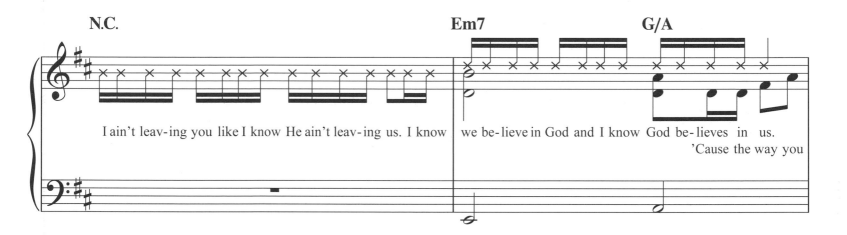

N.C.   **Em7**   **G/A**

I ain't leav-ing you like I know He ain't leav-ing us. I know   we be-lieve in God and I know God be-lieves in us.
'Cause the way you

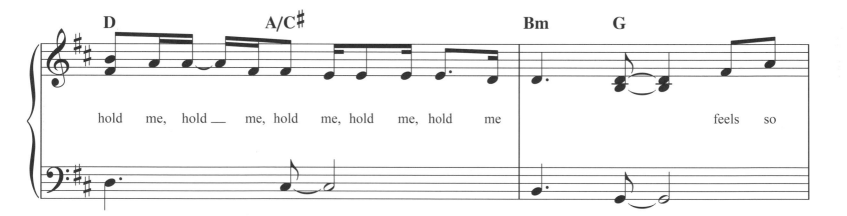

D   **A/C#**   **Bm**   **G**

hold me, hold ___ me, hold me, hold me, hold me   feels so

D   **A/C#**   **Bm**   **G**

ho - ly, ho - ly, ho - ly, ho - ly, ho - ly.   Oh God,

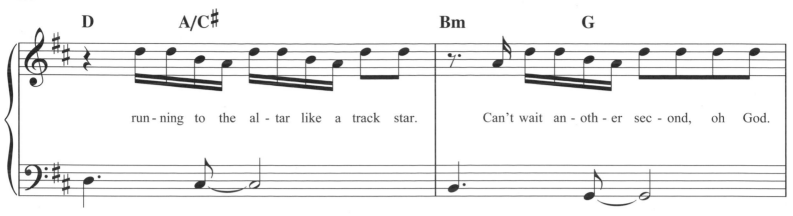

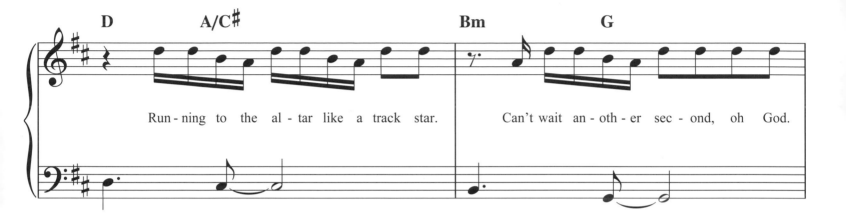

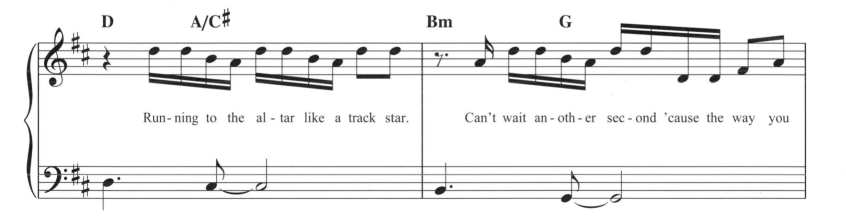

WILLOW

Words and Music by TAYLOR SWIFT
and AARON DESSNER

Moderately, in 2

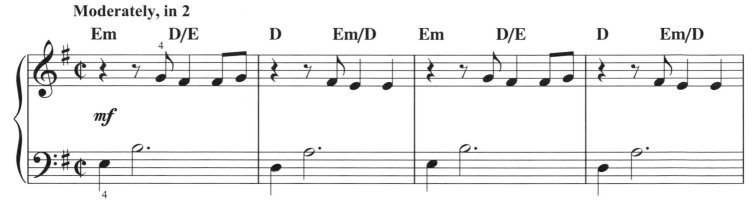

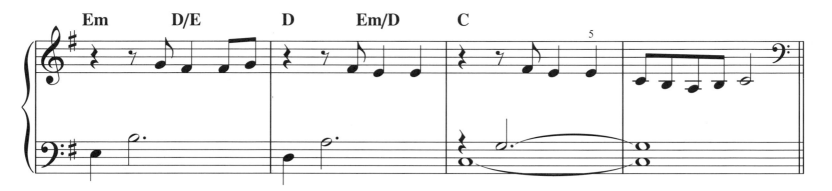

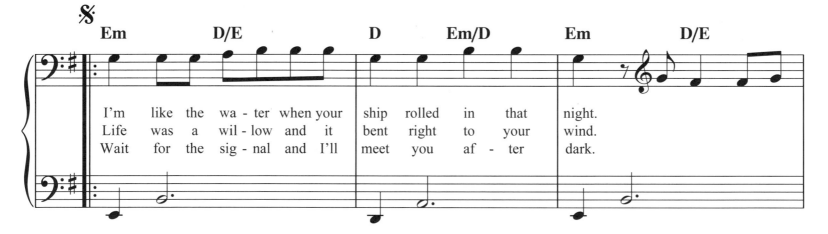

I'm like the wa-ter when your ship rolled in that night.
Life was a wil-low and it bent right to your wind.
Wait for the sig-nal and I'll meet you af-ter dark.

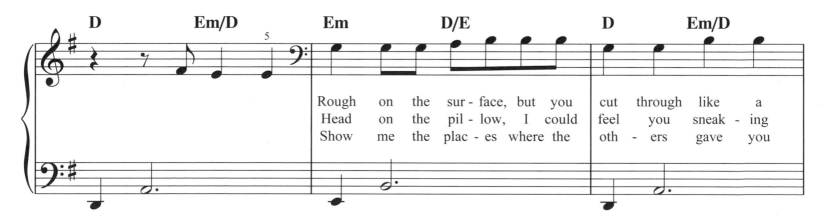

Rough on the sur-face, but you cut through like a
Head on the pil-low, I could feel you sneak-ing
Show me the plac-es where the oth-ers gave you

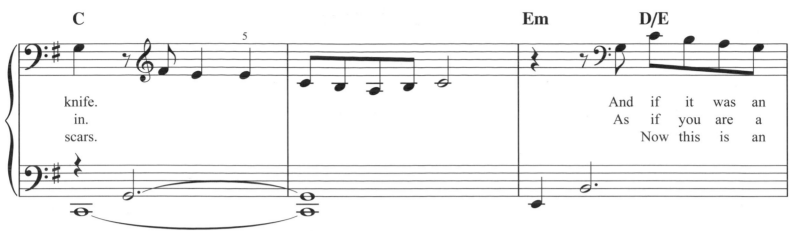

knife.
in.
scars.

And if it was an
As if you are a
Now this is an

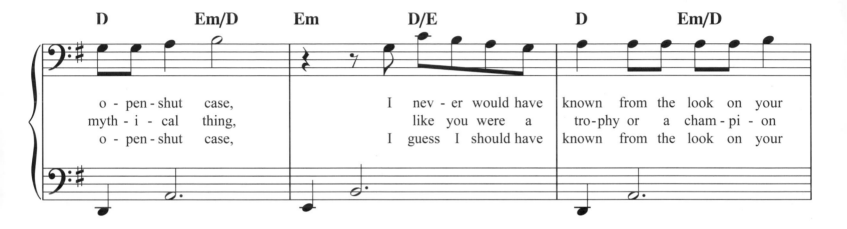

o - pen - shut case,
myth - i - cal thing,
o - pen - shut case,

I nev - er would have
like you were a
I guess I should have

known from the look on your
tro-phy or a cham - pi - on
known from the look on your

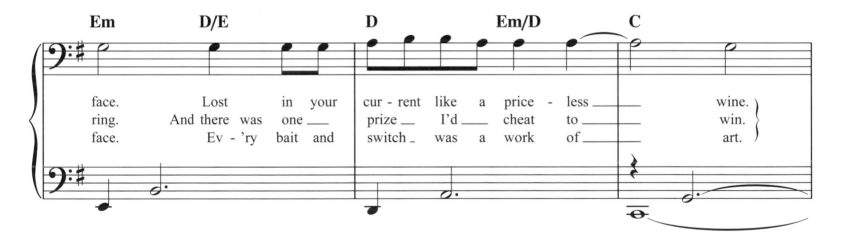

face.   Lost   in your
ring.   And there was one ___
face.   Ev - 'ry bait and

cur - rent like a price - less ___
prize ___ I'd ___ cheat to ___
switch _ was a work of ___

wine.
win.
art.

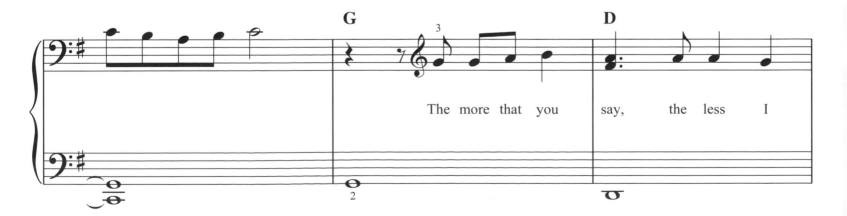

The more that you   say,   the less I

know. Wher - ev - er you stray, I fol - low. I'm beg - ging for

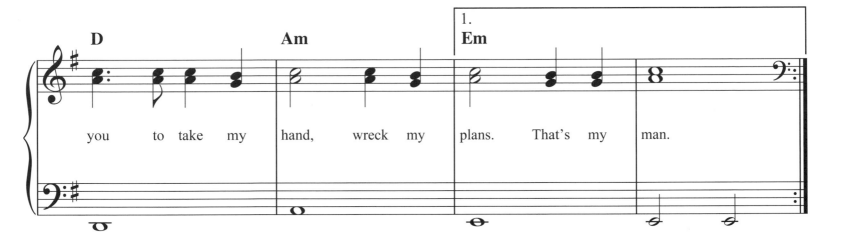

you to take my hand, wreck my plans. That's my man.

plans. That's my man. You know that my train could take you home; an - y-where

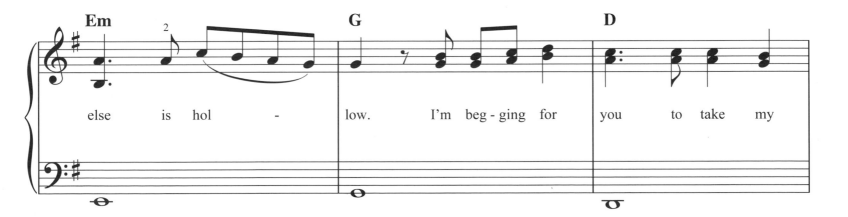

else is hol - low. I'm beg - ging for you to take my

hand,   wreck   my   plans.   That's   my   man.

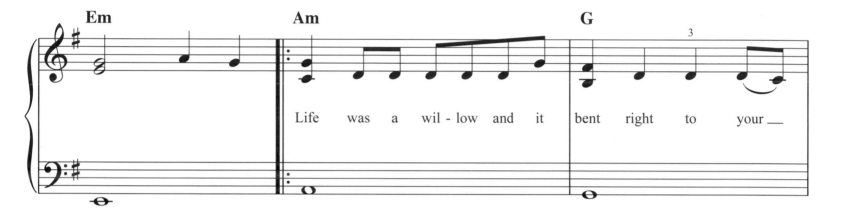

Life   was   a   wil - low   and   it   bent   right   to   your __

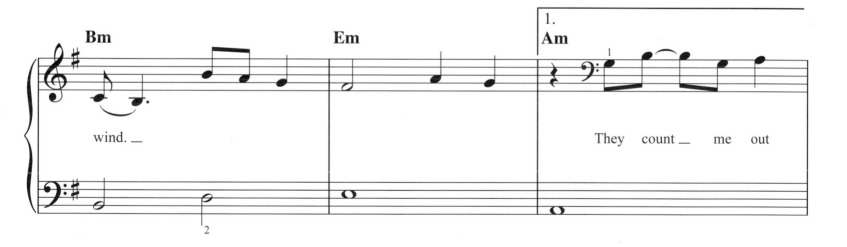

wind. __   They   count __ me   out

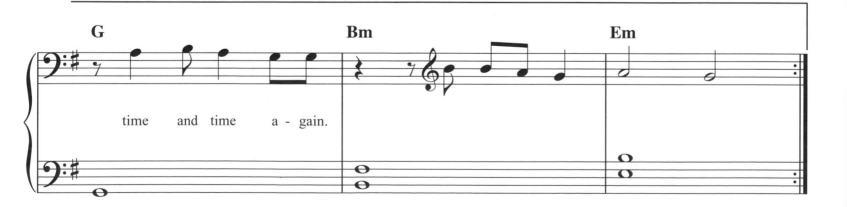

time   and   time   a - gain.

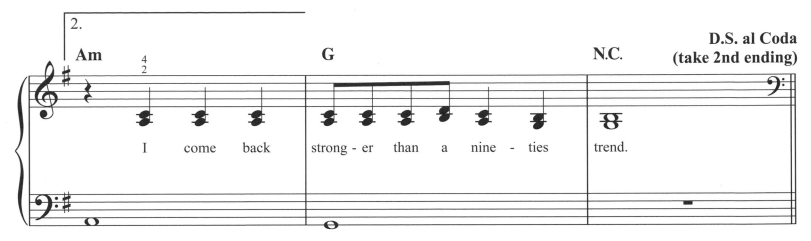

D.S. al Coda
(take 2nd ending)

I come back strong-er than a nine-ties trend.

plans. That's my man. The more that you say, the less I ___

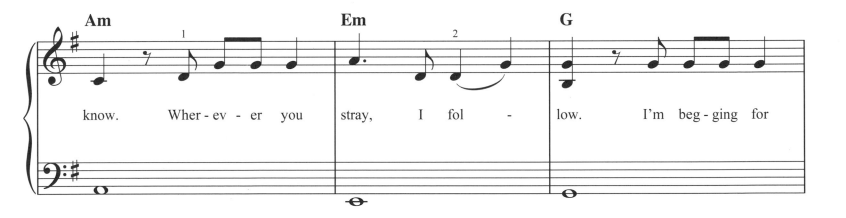

know. Wher-ev-er you stray, I fol - low. I'm beg-ging for

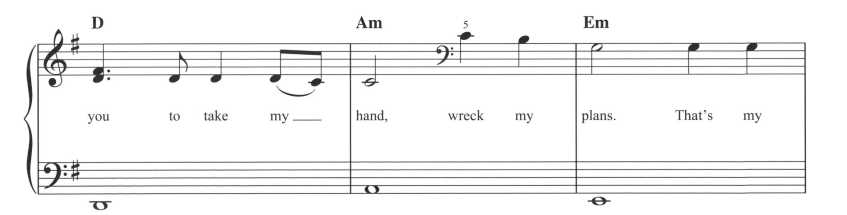

you to take my ___ hand, wreck my plans. That's my

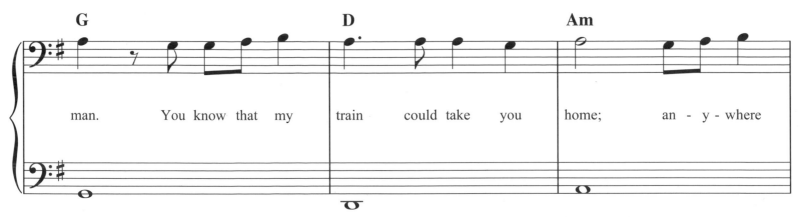

man.　　You know that my train could take you home; an-y-where

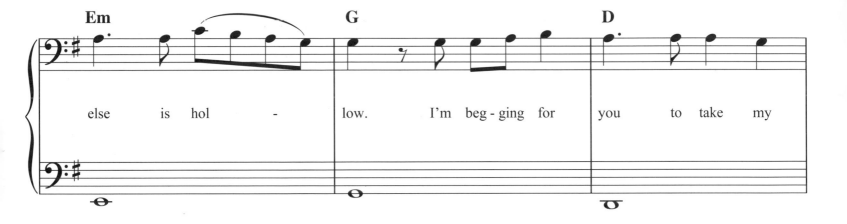

else is hol - low. I'm beg-ging for you to take my

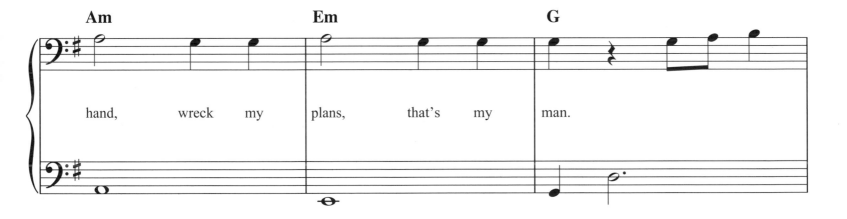

hand, wreck my plans, that's my man.

Hey, __ that's my man. Yeah, that's my

man.　　　　　　　　　　　　　Yeah, that's my　man.　　　　　Ev - 'ry bait and

switch　was　a　work　of　art.　　That's　my　man.

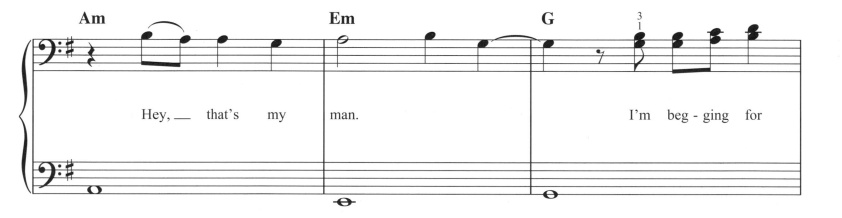

Hey, — that's　my　man.　　　　　　　　I'm beg - ging for

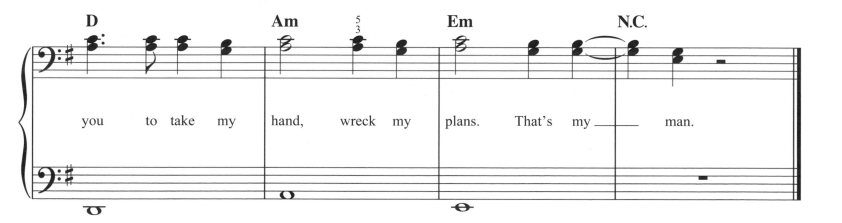

you　to take my　hand,　wreck my　plans.　That's my — man.

POP PIANO HITS

Pop Piano Hits is a series designed for students of all ages. Each book contains five simple and easy-to-read arrangements of today's most popular downloads. Lyrics, fingering and chord symbols are included to help you make the most of each arrangement. Enjoy your favorite songs and artists today!

BELIEVER, WHAT ABOUT US & MORE HOT SINGLES

Attention (Charlie Puth) • Believer (Imagine Dragons) • There's Nothing Holdin' Me Back (Shawn Mendes) • Too Good at Goodbyes (Sam Smith) • What About Us (P!nk).
00251934 Easy Piano. $9.99

BLANK SPACE, I REALLY LIKE YOU & MORE HOT SINGLES

Blank Space (Taylor Swift) • Heartbeat Song (Kelly Clarkson) • I Really Like You (Carly Rae Jepsen) • I'm Not the Only One (Sam Smith) • Thinking Out Loud (Ed Sheeran).
00146286 Easy Piano. $9.99

CAN'T STOP THE FEELING, 7 YEARS & MORE HOT SINGLES

Can't Stop the Feeling (Justin Timberlake) • H.O.L.Y. (Florida Georgia Line) • Just Like Fire (Pink) • Lost Boy (Ruth B.) • 7 Years (Lukas Graham).
00193755 Easy Piano. $9.99

CITY OF STARS, MERCY & MORE HOT SINGLES

City of Stars (from *La La Land*) • Evermore (from *Beauty and the Beast*) • Mercy (Shawn Mendes) • Perfect (Ed Sheeran) • Stay (Zedd & Alessia Cara).
00236097 Easy Piano. $9.99

FEEL IT STILL, REWRITE THE STARS & MORE HOT SINGLES

Feel It Still (Portugal. The Man) • Lost in Japan (Shawn Mendes) • The Middle (Zedd, Maren Morris & Grey) • Rewrite the Stars (from *The Greatest Showman*) • Whatever It Takes (Imagine Dragons).
00278090 Easy Piano. $9.99

GIRLS LIKE YOU, HAPPY NOW & MORE HOT SINGLES

Girls Like You (Maroon 5) • Happy Now (Zedd feat. Elley Duhé) • Treat Myself (Meghan Trainor) • You Are the Reason (Calum Scott) • You Say (Lauren Daigle).
00285014 Easy Piano. $9.99

HOW FAR I'LL GO, THIS TOWN & MORE HOT SINGLES

How Far I'll Go (Alessia Cara - from *Moana*) • My Way (Calvin Harris) • This Town (Niall Horan) • Treat You Better (Shawn Mendes) • We Don't Talk Anymore (Charlie Puth feat. Selena Gomez).
00211286 Easy Piano. $9.99

I DON'T CARE, ME! & MORE HOT SINGLES

I Don't Care (Ed Sheeran & Justin Bieber) • If I Can't Have You (Shawn Mendes) • ME! (Taylor Swift) • Rainbow (Kacey Musgraves) • Someone You Loved (Lewis Capaldi).
00299798 Easy Piano. $9.99

LET IT GO, HAPPY & MORE HOT SINGLES

All of Me (John Legend) • Dark Horse (Katy Perry) • Happy (Pharrell) • Let It Go (Demi Lovato) • Pompeii (Bastille).
00128204 Easy Piano. $9.99

LOVE YOURSELF, STITCHES & MORE HOT SINGLES

Like I'm Gonna Lose You (Meghan Trainor) • Love Yourself (Justin Bieber) • One Call Away (Charlie Puth) • Stitches (Shawn Mendes) • Stressed Out (Twenty One Pilots).
00159285 Easy Piano. $9.99

MEMORIES, TRUTH HURTS & MORE HOT SINGLES

Beautiful People • Lose You to Love Me • Memories • 10,000 Hours • Truth Hurts.
00328173 Easy Piano. $9.99

ROAR, ROYALS & MORE HOT SINGLES

Atlas (Coldplay – from *The Hunger Games: Catching Fire*) • Roar (Katy Perry) • Royals (Lorde) • Safe and Sound (Capital Cities) • Wake Me Up! (Avicii).
00123868 Easy Piano. $9.99

SAY SOMETHING, COUNTING STARS & MORE HOT SINGLES

Counting Stars (One Republic) • Demons (Imagine Dragons) • Let Her Go (Passenger) • Say Something (A Great Big World) • Story of My Life (One Direction).
00125356 Easy Piano. $9.99

SEE YOU AGAIN, FLASHLIGHT & MORE HOT SINGLES

Budapest (George Ezra) • Flashlight (Jessie J.) • Honey I'm Good (Andy Grammer) • See You Again (Wiz Khalifa) • Shut Up and Dance (Walk the Moon).
00150045 Easy Piano. $9.99

SHAKE IT OFF, ALL ABOUT THAT BASS & MORE HOT SINGLES

All About That Bass (Meghan Trainor) • Shake It Off (Taylor Swift) • A Sky Full of Stars (Coldplay) • Something in the Water (Carrie Underwood) • Take Me to Church (Hozier).
00142734 Easy Piano. $9.99

SUNFLOWER, WITHOUT ME & MORE HOT SINGLES

High Hopes (Panic! at the Disco) • No Place (Backstreet Boys) • Shallow (Lady Gaga and Bradley Cooper) • Sunflower (Post Malone) • Without Me (Halsey).
00291634 Easy Piano. $9.99

HAL•LEONARD®

www.halleonard.com

Prices, contents and availability subject to change without notice.

0220
186